THE GREATEST TESTIMONIES OF ALL TIME

V2C networks is a company incorporated in the UK having its registered office in London, Delta. Registered company number: BN: 2371917

Published by V2C NETWORKS 2017

ISBN

Typeset by francis otega

Cover design by Tony Ife

Printed by createspace, an Amazon.com company

I dedicate this book to God, and may these testimonies happen in your lives as you believe in the miraculous hand of God.

INTRODUCTION

I have the privilege of being the pastor of divine mercy ministries for over twenty years. In all those times, the power of God has moved tremendously in this ministry and I have seen with my very eyes the wonders of the most high.

When I was called into this ministry, I asked for a sign that I may see first-hand, the power of God move through me to heal and restore the sick. So in my first crusade in East London, a sick man was brought to me. He had been down suffering from kidney related illness. I didn't know what it was called at the time but I remember it was a kidney problem.

I didn't know what to make of this and I didn't want to be embarrassed. I moved closer to the man as I silently prayed begging God to come to my rescue. I prayed and I heard a voice, which I am used to now, deep inside me, saying, 'my son, go and touch him. I am that I am and it was I who called you to this ministry.'

With the courage of a boy whose father sent him to go and steal, I was moved by the spirit of God to touch him, and lo and behold, he regained strength immediately and moved around the whole place rejoicing. He said later that he was filed with strength that he could lift up an aero plane.

Since that day, I have witnessed first class the wonders of God in this ministry.

Here in this book, I bring to you the best testimonies I have ever heard. I would have loved to give out this book for free, but I don't know how to do this since Amazon's policy require that you attach a price.

Sit back and enjoy this book and see what the lord has done in the lives of people. It is amazing and I pray that the same God who did this for others would do it for you as you key into this testimonies.

You may have been waiting on God's promises, it may tarry, but I tell you, there is light at the end of the tunnel. The God who wiped the tears of Esther and Job, will visit you soon and you will see the wonder working power of God.

Believe and never lose hope. Hold on for Joy comes tomorrow.

I will tell this testimonies the way it was said by the testifiers.

Remember, a closed mouth is a close destiny. Always testify of God's goodness in your life to make it permanent.

1

DELIVERANCE AND TOTAL RESTORATION

Thank you Jesus. What the lord has done for me, I cannot say it all. I have been paralyzed for four years and was to undergo surgery which would cost about $4000.00 for an illness that could not be explained by the doctors. I thought that all hope was lost. I had lost my job and there was no income from anywhere. My wife and children basically lived off my dwindling savings and the benefits I had received from my employers.

I continued praying hoping that this cup will pass over me. So one day, my wife heard of a crusade in one of the churches in Ohio, being a strong believer and a devoted faithful in the church. She insisted that she must take me out of the bed to the church.

At that point, I counted it that she was crazy, but because I had no choice of my own, I allowed her make all the decisions and today I thank God I did not resist like I usually do. I was brought to the camp ground in our family car and was brought in a stretcher provided by the hospital. The doctors must have believed in God to allow all of that. I was taken straight to the altar where I laid with others.

While the service was going on, the man of God which I later knew as Rev. Valentine Hyacinth said so much about life that I thought he knew me from my mother's womb.

All his sermon that day was about me and there I knew I had not been fair to my God. My life was presented before me. I never paid tithes nor went to the congregation of the brethren. I even cheated on my wife severally. I cried when my sins were presented before me.

Then he came to me and gradually led me to Christ. When he touched me and held my hand, I knew that a force that I could not comprehend had entered me. Suddenly I felt strength and power inside of me. I turned around and saw my wife lifting up her hands in praise and when I turned back to look at the reverend, he gradually dragged me up and I started jumping up, something I had never done in years.

My wife came to me in tears holding me and embracing me. For the first time, I held my children again and kissed my wife.

The best part of it all was that I was called to re-take my job with a salary increment and promotion. That is the God that I serve who has delivered me and restored me to his glory. Since that spiritual touch, my life has been that of greatness and I practically beg my children not to deviate from the word of God.

Thank you.

2

MIRACLE JOB AFTER MANY YEARS OF GRADUATION

Praise God, my name is Chris and I am from Nigeria. Reverend, I sent this email so you can know what God has done in my life through your prayer book '120 deliverance and turnaround prayer bullets.'

Everyone knows how Nigeria is and how our leaders has made the entire country difficult and why it is so difficult to get a job.

I graduated here in 2006 and up till 2012 I was still searching for a job. I have been called to many interviews and nothing comes out of it. The situation has bothered my parents so much that I started wondering if I would ever get a job. Many of my mates had moved on in life and here I was, with one of the best results in my class, yet finding it very difficult to get a job. I have gone to nothing less than 250 interviews, but nothing positive came out of it.

When you visited Nigeria, I came to your crusade and was opportuned to buy one of your books, 120 deliverance and turnaround prayer bullets.

 I said that prayer diligently and observed the fastings that was prescribed in the book.

Exactly 21 days later, an application that I made to Shell petroleum some years back was looked into and I was called for an interview.

The beautiful part was that when I got there, the leader of the panel was my class mate whom I had helped severally to solve class work problems.

He was shocked to see that it was me and because he was head of the panel, I was not interviewed, instead we chatted about old times before I left to give room for others. He took me to his office and I stayed there for a while before i left.

Three days later, I was called upon to resume at the administrative block with with a salary beyond what I could explain in writing. Suddenly, I have joined the big league.

Indeed God answers prayers if prayed correctly. Now I recommend this book to every one passing through a difficult time in life.

Praise the lord. Amen.

3

HEALED FROM FIBROID AND MIRACLE BABY

Dear sir, I am Aretha. God has healed me from fibroid during the 21 days fast in the Divine mercy ministry's program of 'operation pharaoh let my people go.' During this program, my mother encouraged me to sow a seed of faith which I did. I sent a text and received a prayer text from the man of God and immediately, I stood like I had not done before and claimed my healing.

I went for another pelvic scan on the 20th of February 2012 and it was confirmed that I didn't have any trace of fibroid in me. Two months later I was confirmed pregnant.

I give God all the glory.

4

SS CHANGED TO AA

Praise the lord. When I had my baby boy in 2009, the joy that filled my heart could not be explained. I say this because I had waited for 9 years before my wife could conceive. So you can imagine the joy that filled our heart.

With it came our problem, that was when we knew that I and my wife were AS carriers. My son was diagnosed with sickle cell anaemia commonly known as hemoglobin SS. My son became so sick that the doctors conducted so many tests before concluding that he only had a few days to live, that his sickle cell disease was very severe.

If the doctors have lost hope, there was nothing else I could do than to take my son to the altar of God. My wife and I are believers and we believe in the power of prayers. She had gone to almost all the prayer groups on facebook asking that her son be healed.

I bought the 120 deliverance and turnaround prayer book and prayed on my son and in the night I would place the book on the chest of my son and go to sleep.

Something tremendous happened on the first day. When I placed the book on him, he stopped crying immediately and slept off. The next day, he woke up looking strong and for the first time, he sucked breast. What a miracle. We kept our hopes high and continued breast-feeding him. My wife was so happy that finally she was breast-feeding her child. I could see the joy on her face. But that was not my problem. I wanted to see my child survive. So at night, before I could come back from work, I saw my wife confessing with the prayer book making sure she finished the entire prayers on my son.

Three days later, our son looked healthier for the first time in his life. I told my wife that we have to go see the doctor for a confirmation that he would be ok, if only for a few more years. She bluntly refused saying that God has healed her son not minding whatever the doctors had to say. Two weeks later, I managed to convince her for a re-test and to glory of God, our son Charles has been confirmed healthy and no trace of the sickle cell could be seen in him.

From that day, my wife and I have grown in faith and no matter what we face as a family, when we call on God of Divine mercy ministry, he answers us and we have come to know that every challenge is for the believer to grow in faith, to fight out his beliefs and salvation.

Praise the lord.

5

THE HOLE IN MY HEART SUDDENLY DISAPPEARED

My name is franklin, a member of the divine mercy ministry in Dublin. I am 28 years old.

When doing a hard task, I usually feel so tired easily, gasping for air and wondering why I could not do many things expected of a young man. This worried me so much that I had to see a doctor.

On examination, it was diagnosed that there was a hole in my heart at the reddington hospital in Dublin. I was devastated but the doctors gave me hope that there was a cure only that I was to go through surgery. I cried to my parents back home in Cork. They started running around to raise the money for the surgery. At the time, I didn't have any insurance and on the second thought, I never wanted to undergo surgery.

The thought of living with the ailment weighed me down and I could do nothing more but resign to fate.

When Rev. Valentine Hyacinth visited Dublin, my mother told me that I must be at the church service. I reluctantly went hoping that my case would be called.

Few minutes into his sermon, he called out my case. Though we were two other people who came out, but at that point I knew I would be healed. Brethren, God touched me in a mysterious way because when he laid his hands on me, the holy spirit moved through me into my entire body and I could feel the power of God working in me.

I could feel my heart in that state and it looked like a hand was cleaning out dirt from it. I suddenly felt cold and the center could no longer hold so I fell down. I laid down for a while and when I woke the man of God had finished his sermon and was in the crowd healing people.

I stood up and left. The next day, I went for another test and I was confirmed healed and even the doctors were baffled and started asking questions. I had no option than to lead them to Christ.

Please join me in thanking God for what he has done for me. Praise the lord.

6

A CASE OF HIV

Praise the lord. My name is Thobanjelo. I am from south Africa. I relocated to the United kingdom about six years ago because I cannot live with the stigma of being HIV positive. I was ashamed of myself and was easily seen as a social outcast. No one wanted to be my friend.

So with the help of my family, I relocated to the United Kingdom so as to start my life afresh. I was introduced to the Divine Mercy ministry by a friend who I met while working in the area of East London as a nanny. I started going to the church.

On the night of 6th July, 2010, Rev. Valentine called out my case, though I was ashamed to come out, I stood where I am and claimed my healing. I bought the 120 deliverance and turnaround prayer book and prayed specially about my case and to the glory of God, I went to see my doctor and after conducting a test, testified that there was no trace of the virus in me and for 6 months now, I have not spent any money on ARVs.

What the lord has done for me, I cannot say it, he has washed my sins and cleansed me from al of my guilt. I will sing and dance and forever praise this God who has wiped my tears from shame. True, there is power in prayer.

7

HE WIPED MY TEARS AND GAVE ME A JOB

I want to appreciate God for what he has done for me. during the fourteen day fasting programme in 2004, on the 9th day to be precise, which was the 14th of march, 2004. The topic of the sermon for that day was, "WHEN HE TAKES TIME." A brother testified of how he got a job after believing Rev. Valentine's prophecy and that provoked me unto goodness and expectation because I was believing God for a job. After the brother's testimony, you prophesized again that there would be a manifestation of miracles of whatever we were believing God for within twenty-eight days.

It may interest you to know that I had been out of work for nearly six months and this has brought untold hardship for me and my family. With so much faith and believe, I keyed into that prophecy.

I quietly wrote on top of that day's devotion 'COUNTING DOWN' and calculated twenty-eight days from that date which was supposed to end on the 11th of April, 2004 and I wrote on top of it 'LAST DAY OF THE MANIFESTATION OF MY JOB.'

To the glory of God, on the 18th day of March, 2004 I was called for an interview and on the 23rd of March, I was called to come for my employment letter that I was successful and I am writing to you, I have resumed work.

God is really and is working mightily t those who believe.

GLORY BE TO GOD.

8

SAVED FROM THE SPIRIT OF DEATH

Dear Rev, I praise the almighty God for delivering my daughter from the spirit of death during last year's fourteen days fasting programme tagged 'CHANGE MY NAME'

My daughter was down with an unknown ailment and has been taken to many hospitals including the prestigious kings college Hospital in London, but I believed that my God would deliver her from that strange illness.

I thank God for obeying your instruction on the 15th of July, 2014 after praying with my 185 prayer bullets for winners in which you asked us to sow some copies into the life of people and that after sowing that we should expect testimonies that will shock us.

I took my about £30 and bought many copies which I shared to many people in my office. That also has its testimony on its own because the people I shared that prayer book to are reaping their benefits from God almighty.

One night during after sharing this prayer book at about 2am, my daughter dreamt that she saw two men, one in suit and another in pure white garment. They said to her, 'my daughter remove what is on your chest,' she answered, 'what is on my chest?' checking her chest.

She saw a lizard come out of her as she woke up screaming. That scream woke everybody up in the house as we all began to praise God after hearing her.

Before this deliverance, all her dreams has always been about death but after that night it has been peaceful and happy dreams. Truly, God has saved my daughter from the spirit of death.

9

HEALED FROM PROFUSE BLEEDING

My God is my tear wiper. He has wiped my tear from an embarrassing disease. Fibroid has dealt with me a dirty blow.

It was so embarrassing that anytime I had my monthly flow, I bled profusely. I visited the divine mercy ministry at the anointing night and that was where I received my miracle.

That night I had my monthly flow so I visited the toilet severally, in fact I visited every 20 minutes to change my pad. The sanitation workers all noticed my frequency to the toilet.

At some point I had to use diapers instead of the normal sanitary pads.

Please thank God for me because in that vast crowd, suddenly the man of God mentioned my case from the pulpit and the bleeding and pain stopped immediately.

I later went for scan and the fibroid had disappeared too. Praise the Lord.

10

JESUS IS MY RULE CHANGER

Brothers and sisters, I praise God for remembering my case. For the past five years, I felt my career was stagnated. My friends all around me were moving from one position to another while others were changing jobs to a higher level, but I was stagnated in the same position all these time.

The july fast brought about a change in my season. I never doubted who God was in my life and what he could do irrespective of the year.

I have been praying to God for a new job and just suddenly one of my applications at a global multinational company called me up and to the glory of God, I secured the job

I felt really humbled to work there and realized that only God could have done that. On my first day at the job, I was told I was promoted to an assistant manager. God himself created a position for me that didn't exist before. He promoted me before I even started the job.

I know to the human mind, this does not make any sense, but only the power of God could change the rules for my sake and fetch water in a basket to shame the bucket. He is my rule changer and forever will be my God.

11

HEALED FROM HALITOSIS

Dear Rev, I want to share my testimony with the world. God has healed my son from halitosis commonly called bad breath which we have been battling since he was a baby.

As we started the fourteen day fasting programme, I asked God to heal my son of it and on the 7th day, there was no smell again.

I praise God who has done it again for me. Thank you Jesus.

12

JEHOVAH, THE FRUIT OF THE WOMB SPECIALIST

Good day sir, I have been waiting on God for years for children. One day, a friend introduced me to 185 prayer bullets for winners and I kept saying those prayer points targeting it all on my childlessness. I read, studied and prayed with it and ensured that I did not miss any prayer point.

I keyed into the numerous prophecies and declarations. As the yearly tradition of 21 and 14 days fasting and prayers came up, I participated again holding on and holding out trusting in God all the way. I kept my promise of holding on to God's promises, always reminding him of his promises.

Exodus 23:26 became my song and I held onto it. I held on to the prophecy of 28000 pregnancies. Then on July 7th, 2012, on my fifth wedding anniversary, I wept and asked God to confirm his word.

Behold in August, my monthly cycle ceased. I held on to the second month, and when I was sure that it was not coming and also due to my body changes, my husband took me to the lab and I was confirmed 6 weeks pregnant and our bundles of Joy came on the April 4th the following year. Yes, God blessed me with a twin, one boy and a girl.

PRAISE THE LORD.

13

SAVED FROM POISON

My name is Mr. Nnamdi chekwube from Nigeria and I live in East London. I travelled home to spend Christmas in my hometown in eastern Nigeria. It was a time for me to meet with my siblings and extended family members that I have not seen in a long time.

When I travelled back to East London by January, 2007, I noticed that I was leaning in weight and I started vomiting heavily. Nothing that I ate stayed. My body suddenly changed to worse. For fear of death, I called my father and he said that I had been poisoned. That it was a common poison that enemies give to people to make them suffer and die.

I had my plans to go back to Nigeria to find a cure, but my father said I should stay in East London and find a cure for there was no cure back home.

I immediately knew that they battle I was facing was greater than I had imagined. So I discharged myself from the university hospital and went to God in prayers. I bought the 120 turnaround and deliverance prayer bullets and prayed my hearts out.

I cried to God to spare my life and take all the glory for this is where he can show his authority over the wickedness of men. I cried to God but I did not observe the fast prescribed in the book due to my health. My friends abandon me thinking I was gone.

My God showed up and fought the battle for me. on my 18th day of praying, I noticed I had excreted something unusual, so I dipped my fingers into the shank to bring out something strange that was tied in a red clothe and since that day I regained my strength.

When I fully recovered, I called my father and told him all about my ordeals and he told me I was strong that the poison usually kills within 21 days.

When my father spread the news that I had survived to the rest of the family, a cousin of mine, Chidi confessed to poisoning my drink alleging that when he asked me for money I refused giving him but spent so much on women.

That also opened my eyes to the wickedness that could be found in the heart of men. Since then I have completely devoted my life to the things of God and have eschewed a lifestyle that would lead me to sin.

I thank God almighty for giving me a second chance.

14
HEALED FROM THE CANCER OF THE NOSE

My name is Vanessa and I am from Indiana. I have been living with a condition that has blocked my right nose for over 3 years.

The condition started when I noticed that there was a growth deep inside my nose. It continued growing to the point of covering my entire right nose. I could not breath with that side of the nose.

The doctors suggested surgery was the only way to remove it but also warned that it was a fifty percent chance of survival.

All of a sudden, I was between life and death. I was watching a programme where the Rev. was ministering on the Tv and there he mentioned my case and urged me to continue blowing out that side of the nose and that within three days, I would be free of cancer.

I did as instructed with the faith my heart could muster and blew my nose. I did this so many times and after the end of the first day, I could feel air pass through that side of the nose. This encouraged me to push on and on the second day when I woke, I could breath with that part of the nose.

On the third day, when I woke, I saw a stone-like membrane on my pillow and wondered what it was and was completely oblivious of the fact that I was completely healed of the cancer because I could breathe normally again.

It took me about 15 seconds to remember I was in the hospital. When I found out that the membrane I was holding was the growth in my nose, I shouted for joy which alerted the nurses.

Within minutes, my ward was filled with nurses and doctors who joined me to thank God after hearing my testimony.

Praise God for I have been free from cancer and I am living my normal life again.

15

HEALED FROM PROSTATE CANCER.

Dear Rev. Valentine, I was diagnosed with prostate cancer in the winter of 2007 and since then I was hospitalized and was to undergo surgery.

I told God in prayer that he should spare my life and heal me from the sickness. I was too young to be diagnosed of this ailment at the age of 36.

I cried to God in prayers and expected a miracle from him. when the appointment came, the doctors conducted another test and to the glory of God, the cancer had gone and I have regained my health.

This is a miracle to me and now I urinate without stress. I do not deserve this miracle but God spared me. if he can do this for me, then be rest assured that he can do that for you and anyone who puts his trust in him.

16

FINANCIAL BREAKTHROUGH

I was born in abject poverty and lived in a village in the eastern part of Nigeria. I grew up not knowing what formal education is. I struggled financially all through life until that day I met Christ.

When I accepted him in the crusade of 2001, I made an effort to know more of him and he has continuously revealed himself to me.

I asked for one thing and that was to take my family and I out of this abject poverty.

I was in the business of public transportion but I had no capital to increase my fleet and the one I was using was not really in a good condition. I prayed God for the capital to get a new one and also to increase my fleet.

Because I was diligent in my savings, the bank granted me a soft loan which I used to get a new bus. 10 years later, as I am standing here, I have over 100 buses plying the city of Lagos and my families, both immediate and extended are all doing well and poverty cannot remember if it ever lived amongst us.

To God I give all the glory.

17

CURED FROM LIVER CIRRHOSIS

I was diagnosed with liver cirrhosis in 2010 and since then my health went on the down turn. I was always in and out of the hospital.

I was introduced to the 185 prayer bullets for winners by my sister and I I prayed it continuously believing that the God I had worshipped all my life will deliver me and set me free.

I stayed home and continued to believe God observing my fast. To God's glory, I am completely healed from this disease and I urge you all who have not bought this great book to do so that you may know how to fight the fiery darts of the enemy. Praise God.

18

RAISED FROM THE DEAD

Dear Rev. Valentine, my wife was diagnosed with breast cancer which was at a late stage. This has eaten deep into her health.

I believe the doctors in Africa did not do a thorough job. I had spent a lot of money on chemotherapy and this was not going down well with my wife.

I saw my once very beautiful wife looking so lean and weak, I prayed God to heal her but her condition worsened. The doctors told me in private that there was nothing else they could do for me.

This baffled me. I wondered who my wife was going to abandon five children to take care of alone. I went to God in prayers and asked that he spared my wife.

One morning when I went to see my wife, I entered and found her so weak. She tried to tell me something but no words could come out and before my very eyes my wife breathed her last and died.

I called the doctors and nurses and when they came, they pushed me aside and tried to bring her back but she was gone and before me the nurses tried to cover her face with a cloth to prepare her for the mortuary.

I don't know where I got the strength. In fact, I was not the one speaking because in that condition, I told them that I wanted to be alone with my wife. The nurses called in the doctor, and when he heard my reason allowed me a moment with my wife.

I removed the 120 deliverance and turnaround prayer bullets and placed on the body of my wife. I prayed silently and asked God to prove himself.

Then looking at my wife, I pointed to her and said, "I have not given you the authority to die. You are under me because Christ made it so and the authority over your life rests with me and you cannot die now. By the authority bestowed upon me as your husband and by the power of the God of Divine mercy Ministry, I say rise up now."

To my surprise, my wife's right finger moved and I checked her pulse and it was beating so I rushed down to call the doctors who were dumbfounded to find her alive.

She was resuscitated and to God's glory she is healed of cancer and is now taking care of our children. Faith works brethren and always strive to put it to work.

I thank God again.

19

DELIVERED FROM MARINE WORLD

Dear Rev. my name is Martha and I am Isienu in the south-eastern part of Nigeria. I relocated to east London about three years ago. I am supposed to come out to testify of God's goodness, but I am ashamed I may be stigmatized.

I left Nigeria because I have been married three times and in those marriages, my three husbands died under mysterious circumstances and therefore I became a social outcast. No one wanted to associate with me for fear of death.

Before I even got married, I realized that even all the boys that I slept with in the name of fornication also died mysteriously. This worried me until I found the reason for their deaths when I turned 21.

I was in my sleep and dreamt of a very handsome fair man making love to me, it looked so real that I relaxed and really enjoyed the love-making.

When he was done, he introduced himself as Mkhiya, the prince of Thaca, lord of the seven seas and that he was married to me in this world and in the world to come. He explained to me that it was he who killed all the boys I had sex with and that he was a jealous lover.

He visited me every night and in the same fashion made very sweet love to me. I was now expecting him every night of my life. I got so used to him that when he didn't visit, I take it out on him any other time he comes.

He provided me with everything. I got the best job and was riding the best cars back home. This in turn attracted many suitors. I was now under pressure by my parents to get married.

For fear of Mkhiya, I turned down many eligible suitors, but for fear and respect of my parents, I decided to marry one. Though I knew what was going to happen to him because Mkhiya warned that he would kill them.

The first died in a motor accident along the Lagos-Benin expressway three months after marriage. The second died in another accident along Lagos Ibadan expressway two months after marriage and the third died three weeks after marriage after eating an unexplained poison.

I stopped sleeping with Mkhiya and he made me lose all I have ever received from him. the job, the car and even lost my father. I was determined to stop him from coming to me but I really didn't know who to talk to.

I had to run away. All the churches I visited could not help me. So, when I got to east London, I started visiting the Divine mercy Ministry. On the 8th of July, 2014, during the 14 days fasting for deliverance, I specifically asked God to deliver me.

When my case was called out by you during that crusade, even though about four of us came out, I knew the call was for me.

If only people can remember what actually happened then at the arena. I was the one person that the Rev. spent hours trying to deliver. Mkhiya completely refused to let me go. In the spirit, it was a battle, my spiritual children didn't also want me to go, but I was determined to get free from all of these embarrassments. When the Rev. spits fire and water on me, the whole Kingdom of Darkness goes up in flames and this battle continued until I saw Mkhiya's weakness. He cried and had to let me go. When I opened my eyes to this world again, I knew I was set free. Today, I am happily married to a Nigerian who also worships here and he is a devoted Christian who has encouraged me to testify of God's goodness in my life. Today, I am free from Mkhiya and the kingdom of darkness. Praise the Lord.

20

BLESSED WITH TRPLETS AFTER18 YEARS OF MARRIAGE

Rev, my name is Bridgett and I was married for 18 years without a child. I kept praying and believing God for a miracle even when my menopause was fast approaching.

My mother-in-law gave me the 120 deliverance and turnaround prayer bullets which I used to pray with. It was a wonder. I remember one prayer point which I prayed without ceasing, taking from Psalm 34:10 that "I shall not want any good thing in this marriage. There shall be cry of children in my home." I prayed the Holy Ghost to visit my womb.

I got pregnant but unfortunately got a miscarriage, but the Holy Spirit gave me an assurance that there was something greater that was coming. I became steadfast in prayers and waited upon the lord.

When I got pregnant again, I had an accident and when I was taken to the hospital, I told the doctor that I was pregnant when he wanted to inject me. so they took me to the ultra-sound room and the doctor came out with the coldest verdict I had ever heard in my life, "Woman, there is no pregnancy."

It shocked me to my marrows and I cried to my mother-in-law. I thank God for giving me such a mentor in a mother-in-law. She immediately went in prayers and told me never to lose hope and that the baby was there.

I kept on praying and believing that the pregnancy was still intact. I went to another ultra-scan and they told me that the baby was a retained product, whatever that meant, and that I should flush it out.

"NO," I said and continued praying to God. When I was 3 months gone, I went to the doctors again and after the test, the doctor said, "Where did you go to pray, because what I am seeing here is baffling, I can see three babies dancing."

My joy knew no bounds and on the 6th of March, 2014, I was delivered of two boys and a girl. I thank God for his mercies upon my life. I want to encourage all of you to say no to opposition and believe in the report of the almighty God.

21

DELIVERED FROM MARINE POWERS

My name is Rebecca and I am from Benin in the south of Nigeria. My daughter Rukevwe has been failing her high school exams and this has greatly worried me. I consulted the marine goddess and offered sacrifices of Rice, beans, palm oil, live chicken and other things as demanded by the chief priest of the river. Then I was told to maintain the sacrifice for as long as I lived.

My daughter passed the exams and I offered the sacrifice for two more years then stopped. My daughter passed her exams and graduated as an engineer and later married.

After her marriage, tears were the order of the day because she could not have children and sometimes menstruated four times in a month. She became barren for many years and the husband threatened to send her home.

When we came for your first crusade in Nigeria, you mentioned her case and asked that she used the 120 deliverance and turnaround prayer bullets to pray and constantly place the book on her tummy. This she did for 21 days and to glory of God, her battles ended and she delivered of a baby boy a year later.

TO GOD BE THE GLORY.

22

UNMERITED FAVOUR

Dear Rev., my name is Emmanuel, I am from Jamaica and I live in east London. I have been struggling since I graduated from the university and out of the love I have for a woman, I got married and my real troubles started.

I could not provide for my wife, but though she understood, I felt so ashamed of being called a husband. I prayed every day of my life, but since I started attending the divine mercy ministry, my life changed as I prayed with the 185 prayer bullet for winners.

I was walking along central London one day when I met my lecturer and when I got the car working, he started talking about a new mechanical breakthrough which I was conversant with. I made an impression and in a matter of days, I was introduced to the dean of the faculty of Engineering in the University of London, and within minutes, I was offered a job as an assistant lecturer. Today, I can take care of my wife and daughter.

Praise Master Jesus, Amen.

www.ingramcontent.com/pod-product-compliance
Lightning Source LLC
Chambersburg PA
CBHW071314280526
45788CB00004B/1896